To Melissa
Remember your
Dream. xoxo + Press On,
Tara

The Dream

by Tara Rice Simkins

---------------------------- 〰〰 ----------------------------

art by Leah Campbell Badertscher

Published by
NewFire Publishing
43 Crystal Lake Drive, Suite 200
North Augusta, SC 29860

Visit our website at newfirepublishing.com.

preface

Writing this story was a gift to me which I want to share with you.

When my son, Nat, was 4 1/2 years old, he awoke in a panic one morning and anxiously announced that he "lost his dream." Starting under his bed, we combed the entire house for his dream, but we never found it. This loss weighed heavily on Nat for weeks. Where could his dream be?

One day, three years later, I was driving Nat home from football practice. I am not sure why, but while we were driving, I remembered that morning when Nat had lost his dream. So, I asked Nat whether he remembered that day.

He quickly responded, "Yes."

We drove a few more blocks in silence. Then, he added, "The funny thing is Mommie that I don't think it was ever really lost. We just forgot to look inside me."

It took me two more years to decipher the wise words of this child. This book contains the story that I learned -- what Nat already knew and what he taught me.

I originally intended *The Dream, as Lost and Found by Nat* to be a children's picture book, a lyrical bedtime story which parents could read to their children. I envisioned children sitting in their parents' laps while they read the story together. What I didn't realize until a very talented literary agent pointed it out to me was that the book's audience was not children at all, but mothers. She was right. I had always pictured a tired mom, just like me, picking up this book and finding something in it which reminded her of a time when she used to dream.

The gift in this book, however, is not the words.

The gift in this book is the invitation to explore the stillness in the space between the words. Like the stillness in between an inhale and an exhale. The stillness where dreams are created.

The gift in this book is Leah's art. Her images invite us to explore their layers and their texture. Her images invite us to rest on a curve, or a color. Her images invite us to look deeper still. To dare to dream.

Take a moment to meditate on each of Leah's beautiful prints and to imagine the wind gently calling to you. What do you see? What do you hear? What do you remember?

The gift of this book is that you picked it up and considered, even if only for a moment, the invitation to join us on this journey into stillness and to remember your dreams.

And for that gift to us, we thank you.

XOXO + Press on,

Tara

"Be still and know that I am God." Psalm 46:10

This is the story of a boy and his Dream.

Each night while the boy slept, he dreamed.

He dreamed about a Garden with two beautiful trees, a flowing river and many wonderful animals.

The boy loved his Dream, and he loved being in the Garden where he climbed its trees, skipped rocks in its river and ran with its animals.

And each morning, when the boy opened his eyes, he always remembered his Dream.

During these days, the boy played and spent time with his Mother in peaceful silence by the tree in the garden next to their house where the wind blew, gently.

And the boy carried his Dream within him wherever he went.

As the boy grew, his interests grew. He
enjoyed time with his friends, played football
and went to school.

The boy and his Mother spent more and
more time running from here to there,
and less and less time by the tree in the
garden next to their house where
the wind blew, gently.

And at night, the boy lay in bed wondering,
"What will I be when I grow up?"

"A doctor?"

"A coach?"

"A football star?"

And he slept without dreaming.

One morning the boy awoke and realized
that he had not dreamed about the Garden
with its two beautiful trees, its flowing river
and its wonderful animals.

The boy had lost his Dream.

He looked under his pillow. He looked
under his bed. He looked everywhere.

But he could not find his Dream.

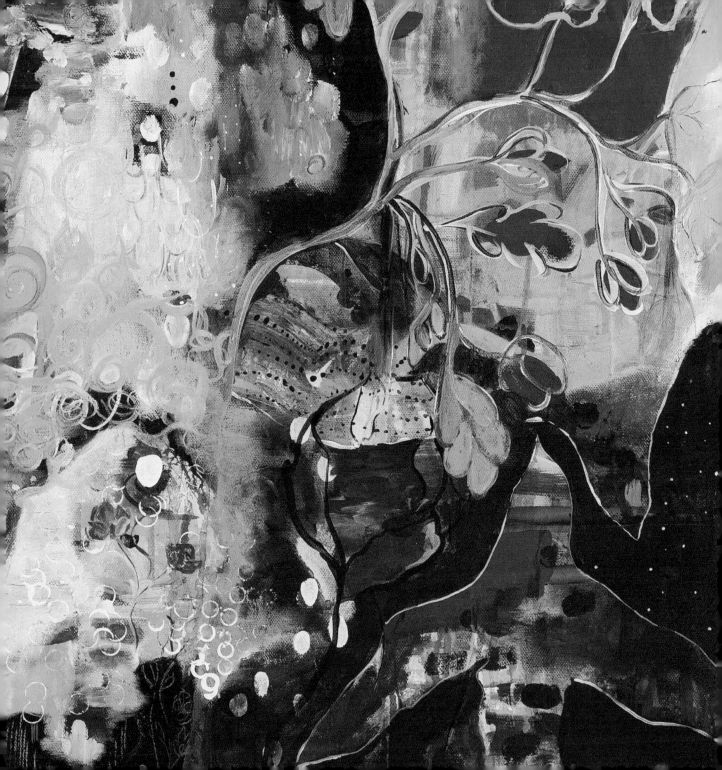

Frantically, the boy called to his Mother, "Mommie, Mommie come quick," and he crawled back under the bed to look for his Dream once more.

Startled, his Mother ran to his room where she found the boy under his bed muttering, "Where did it go? Where did it go?"

The Mother asked, "My dear boy, what is wrong?"

The boy looked up from under the bed, "Mommie, Mommie, I have lost my Dream! I cannot find it anywhere!"

The Mother sighed. Her hands fell to her sides. The corners of her eyes and her mouth dropped. She pulled the boy out from under the bed. Then, she took him in her arms, bent over, lovingly kissed him and whispered, "Be patient. You will find your Dream again, one day."

While she hugged her boy, the Mother was struck by how tired she felt, running here and there. And, she longed for time with the boy by the tree in the garden next to their house where the wind blew, gently.

Days turned into months, and months turned into years, and the boy kept on with the hustle and bustle of life all the while searching for his Dream.

One day tired from the everyday world
and the searching, the boy, now a young
man, returned home to find his
Mother in the garden.

While the boy waited for his Mother,
he decided to rest under the tree in the
garden next to the house where the
wind blew, gently.

In the peaceful silence of the moment,
everything was still, except the wind.

The boy sat and listened. He closed his
eyes, felt the wind against his face, and
began to breathe.

And his Dream returned.

He climbed the trees in the Garden, skipped
rocks in its river, and ran with its animals, as
if he had never left.

The hustle and bustle of the everyday
world with all of its distractions, interactions,
preoccupations and adventures faded
away in the stillness.

The boy was not sure how long he had been climbing trees, skipping rocks and running in the Garden when he heard his mother call, "My boy, I am finished with my digging and my planting. Please join me inside for a snack."

The Mother and the boy sat at the kitchen table, drank tea, ate cookies, laughed and talked.

The Mother asked the boy, "Do you remember the day you lost your Dream?"

The Mother giggled, "You were frantic! I remember that I found you looking under your bed and muttering 'Where did it go? Where did it go?'"

The boy shook his head and smiled, "Yes, Mommie, I remember." Then, the boy shared his new discovery, "Mommie, I found the Dream.

Today, while I was resting under the tree waiting for you to finish digging and planting, the Dream returned!"

The boy paused and added, "Mommie, I think the Dream was inside me the whole time. I just forgot to look there."

The Mother was overjoyed.

She smiled. The boy smiled. Then the Mother said, "The greatest thing about forgetting is …"

And the boy finished her sentence, "remembering!"

This time the boy took his Mother in his arms, bent over and lovingly kissed her.

The boy came back to the tree in the garden next to the house where the wind blew, gently, for the rest of his life.

Upon each return, the hustle and bustle of everyday life faded in the stillness.

The boy climbed the trees in the Garden, skipped rocks in its river and ran with its animals as he had always done from the beginning.

And the boy never lost his Dream again because he carried the Dream within him wherever he went.

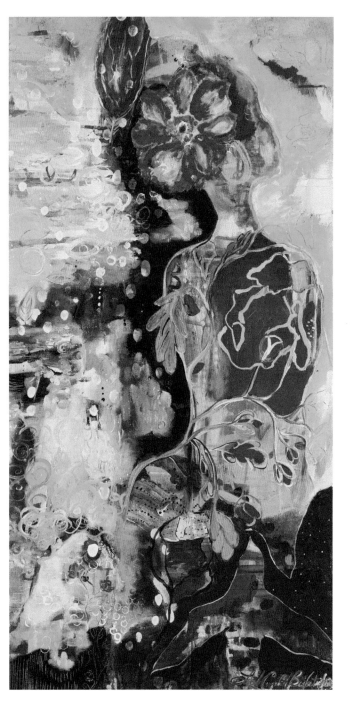

the art

Proverbs says, "without a vision the people perish," and so I agree with those that believe the highest calling of any artist, writer, poet, leader is not only to observe the world and report what has happened and what they see currently, but to also open themselves up to divine energy that is trying to come into the world in order that they may then craft a vision that can, through various mediums, be communicated to others. This seems like a very tall order. On some levels it is. It requires a great commitment to practicing your craft and it requires tremendous vulnerability and courage if you are going to share your dream and your work with the world.

But there is also a piece of this that requires a really wonderful self-forgetting. To help place myself in this good space, I begin every painting with a ritual that includes the same prayer, Dear God - Please help me to remember that I am the vessel and not the source. Please help me to let "me" get out of the way and just be present and respond fully to what wants to happen.

This takes so much pressure off me and, I believe, opens me and my work to possibilities that transcend what I'd be capable of on my own. On the best days, if I'm able to let go of fear and perfectionism, I feel like the process of painting is a triaxial conversation - there's my soul, God, and the medium (paint). The results are far more interesting, fun, and meaningful experiences and paintings than what I could've created on my own.

Rather than beginning with a end-goal in mind for the painting, I work myself into a place of flow as much and as consistently as I can. I know that I'm in the right place when I'm in love with what's happening, no matter what's happening on the canvas. That is, I'm loving the process whether the painting "looks good" or is at an "ugly" or "awkward" stage. If I start to tighten up and worry about that ugliness, then I just remind myself that my work in those moments is to shift into a place of truly loving

what is. If I have an urge to paint with florescent orange, I might notice my mind hesitating but I try to return to honoring and responding fully to the intuition, which I trust is coming from a deeper place, to paint in neon. If I have an area that I think is really pretty good and all of a sudden I want to paint over it with something different, I work to respond fully to that impulse, too. More times than not, having the courage and trust to let go of something I like creates a space for something with much more richness and depth to flow through.

On a very personal and humble level, I've experienced engaging my imagination (dancing that triaxial waltz) and being creative through the medium of painting to be profoundly healing. It's been my experience that there is great joy rising in the world, so much more love that wants to come into the world, and the more I allow myself to turn and face my personal suffering as well as the pain and suffering happening across the planet, the more burning and strong my desire to do whatever I am called to do - painting, coaching, motherhood - from a place of deep love and peace. It is a small thing, but it's my hope that if I am connected to truth when I paint, then whatever I am experiencing - wholeheartedness, courage, joy, love, the release of grief and pain- will somehow be imparted to you, the viewer. I paint because it allows me to put myself in the flow of love and truth and that makes me feel so alive. But I also paint because I believe that the grace that flowed through my experience will be continued on through whoever I am able to share my work and that together we can all be channels for these rising tides of joy and love to wash through the world.

tara rice simkins

Tara Rice Simkins, J.D., is a Certified Life Coach/ Blogger (tarasimkins.com), a co-founder of The Press On to CURE Childhood Cancer Fund of CURE Childhood Cancer (pressonfund.org) and a lawyer (hullbarrett.com).

Tara combines her experience as a life coach and lawyer with her experience as the mother of a childhood cancer survivor to deliver a much needed message for women in today's world. Her family's amazing journey inside the world of pediatric cancer brought Tara to her knees. Literally. Tara shares with her clients, readers and audiences a unique understanding of what it means to potentially lose something very meaningful in your life, and in the face of such loss to commit to living an extraordinary life. Tara's message is simple: "We can always decide to fall deeper into love with our lives and to summon the courage to press on no matter what." Her signature line, "XOXO + Press on," sums up her life philosophy.

Tara lives in North Augusta, South Carolina with her husband, Turner, her three sons, Nat, Brennan and Christopher, and their dog, Lucky.

To learn more about Tara's coaching practice, classes, speaking engagements and other books, please visit tarasimkins.com

leah campbell badertscher

Leah Campbell Badertscher, J.D., is a Certified Life Coach/Blogger (leahrenascence.blogspot.com), writer, and artist (leahcb.com). Leah is also the founder of RENASCENCE CO., a coaching and creativity consulting company dedicated to helping others create, live, and love the life they are meant to with integrity, meaning, and peace.

Years ago, while outwardly appearing to have the perfect life, Leah experienced the life-changing gift of a severe depression. Her experience taught her that the opposite of depression was not happiness, but aliveness and love. From that time on, Leah began to shed old ideas about "success" and "happiness" and committed to learn all she could about living more fully alive from a place of truth and love. She has since come to believe that a strong connection to one's inner voice, an abiding trust in God and your highest purpose, and consciously choosing love for yourself and others- moment by moment, situation by situation, again and again - are key elements in cultivating a meaningful and beautiful life, from the inside-out. Through her art, writing, personal coaching, workshops and retreats, Leah holds a space and shares tools and practices that invite others to connect to their own inner voice, strengthen their intuition, and experience greater aliveness and love.

Leah lives in South Bend, Indiana with her husband, Brad, her two sons, Elijah and Samuel, and their twenty-five pound guard cat, Bud. Leah and her currently all-boy crew are joyfully awaiting a baby girl, due to arrive this summer. To learn more about Leah's coaching work and the art that appears in this book, visit leahcb.com.

"The anchor of the Universe is located within every one of us."

Lao-Tzu

19121238R00019

Made in the USA
Charleston, SC
07 May 2013